LIVELY UKULELE TUNES

ONDŘEJ ŠÁREK

Cedar Solid Top Concert Ukulele CDST-C cover image courtesy of Lanikai Ukuleles.

© 2020 by Mel Bay Publications, Inc. All Rights Reserved.
WWW.MELBAY.COM

Preface

This is a collection of 38 lively, up-tempo tunes arranged for ukulele. Backup chords and tablature are included. Included in this collection are fiddle tunes, reels, hornpipe jigs, sea chanteys, bluegrass and old-time melodies and some original compositions by William Bay. These tunes are ideal for improving technique or just having fun playing the ukulele. So pick up your uke, sit back and enjoy performing these timeless and new melodies.

    Ondřej Šárek

Index of Tunes

Title	Page
American Hornpipe	50
Bill Cheathum	4
Billy in the Lowground	5
Black and White Rag	10
Blanchard's Hornpipe	24
Bottom of the Punch Bowl Hornpipe	25
Brunswick Dance	27
Cape Cod Reel	28
Catawissa Reel	30
Cold, Frosty Morning	6
Devil's Dream	31
Dixie Breakdown	20
East Tennessee Blues	12
Echo Canyon	29
Haste to the Wedding	36
Haul Away, Joe	32
Hens in the Kitchen	37
High Barbaree	40
Hooker's Hornpipe	38
Indian Creek	26
Jacks Fork Rendezvous	23
Katie Trail	39
Lady's Fancy	34
League Reel	8
London Hornpipe	42
Lonesome River	44
Lost Indian	21
Maddie's Bonnet	43
Martha's Cider	45
Powder Mill	49
Rickett's Hornpipe	47
Ships are Sailing Reel	46
Silver Bell	14
Soppin' the Gravy	7
Stone's Rag	16
Sugar in the Gourd	22
Sweet Lillie	18
The Wild Mare	48

Bill Cheathum

Billy in the Lowground

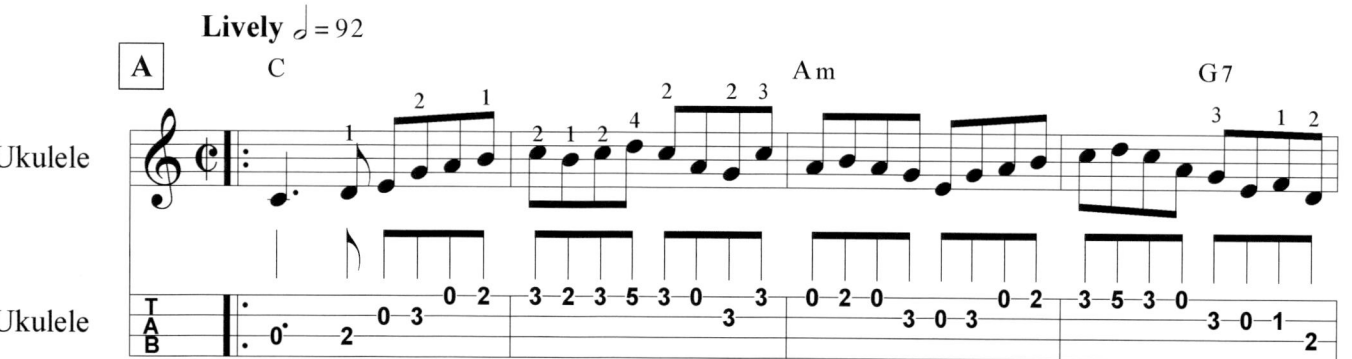
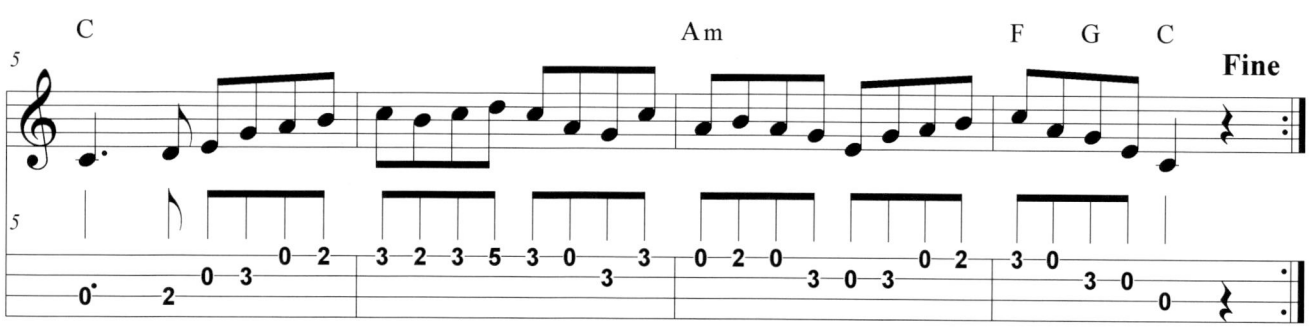
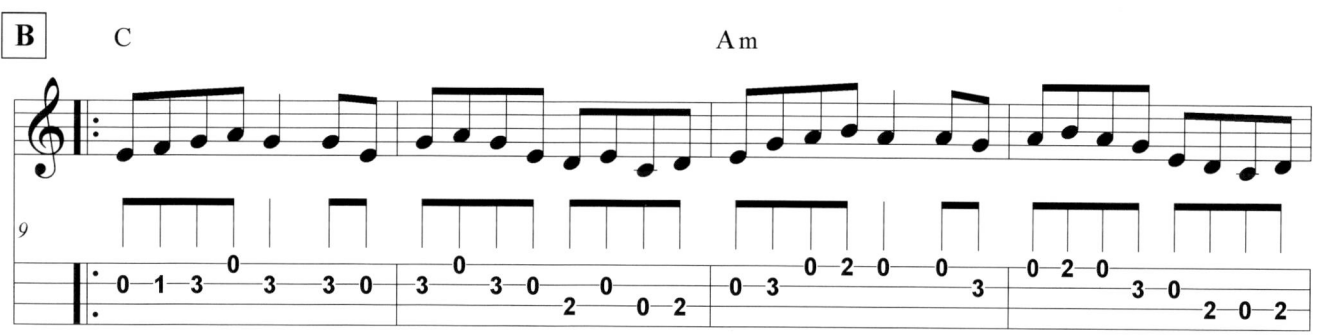
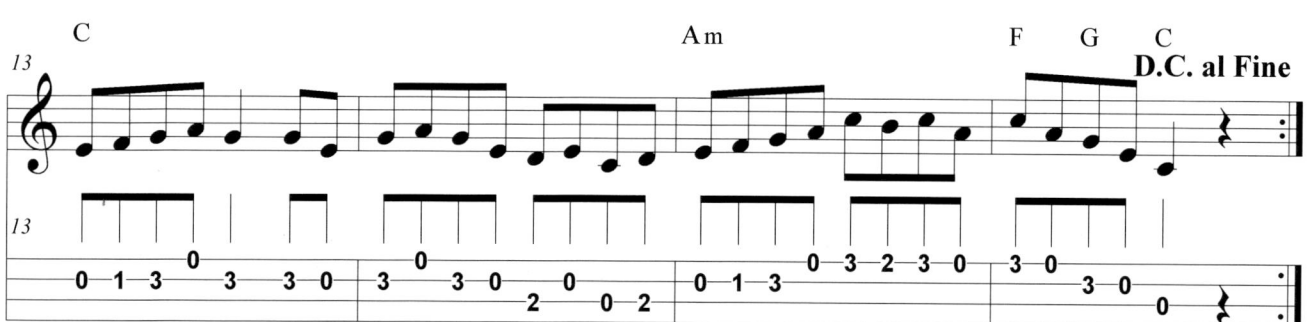

Cold, Frosty Morning

American Fiddle Tune

Soppin' the Gravy

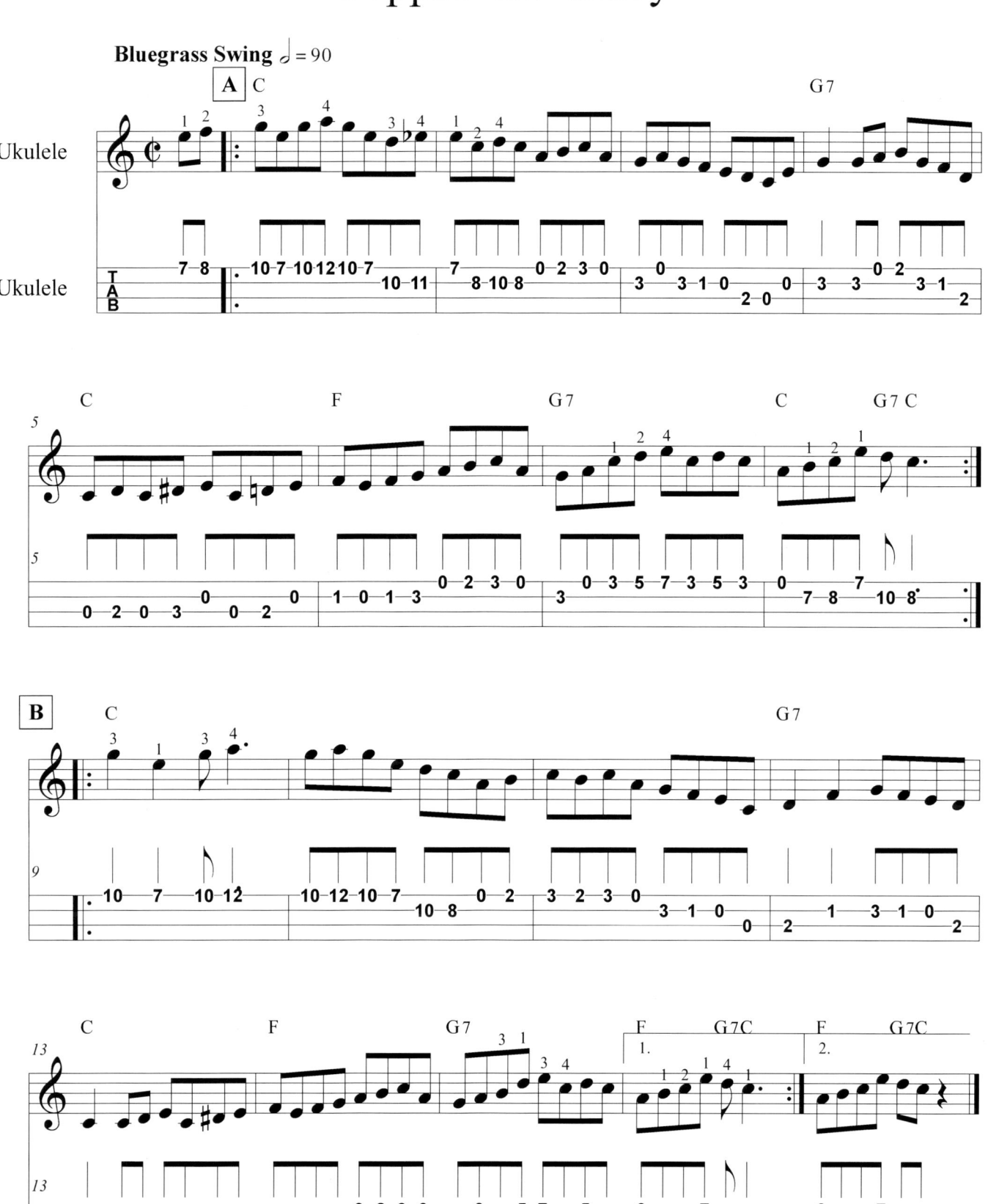

League Reel

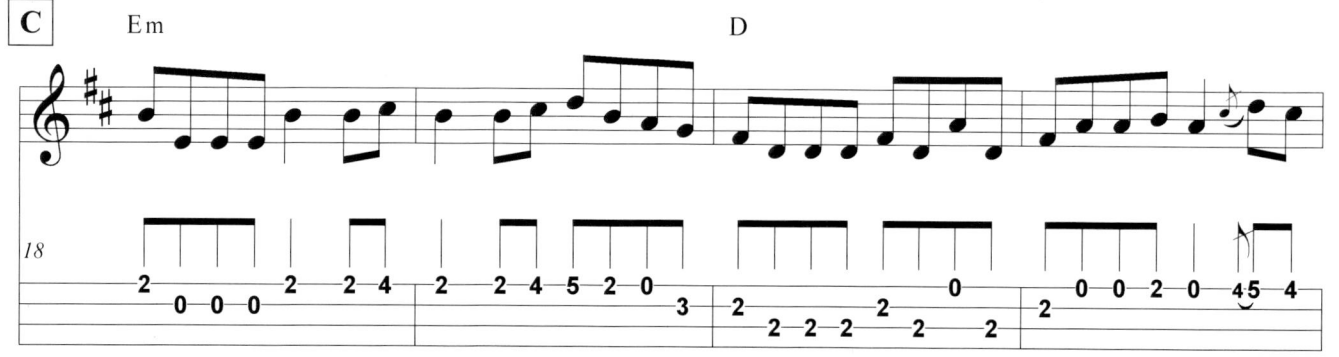
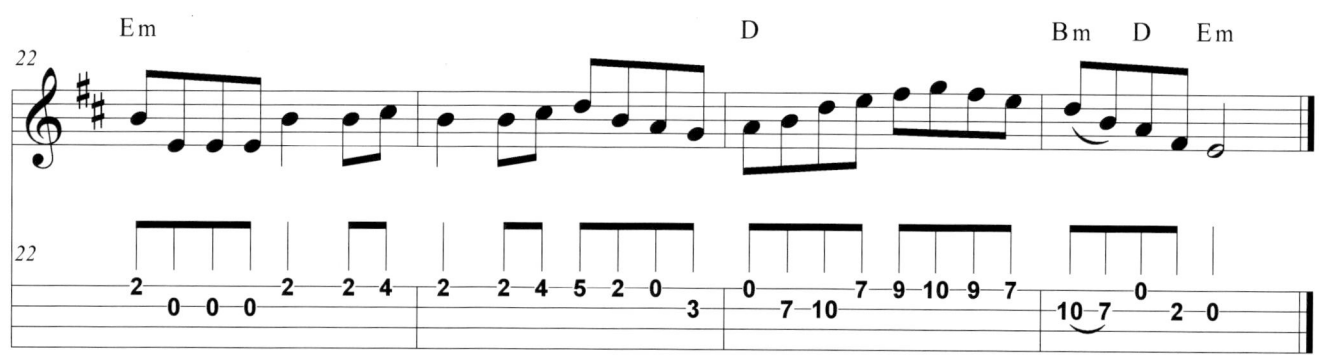

Black and White Rag

Ragtime Swing ♩ = 80

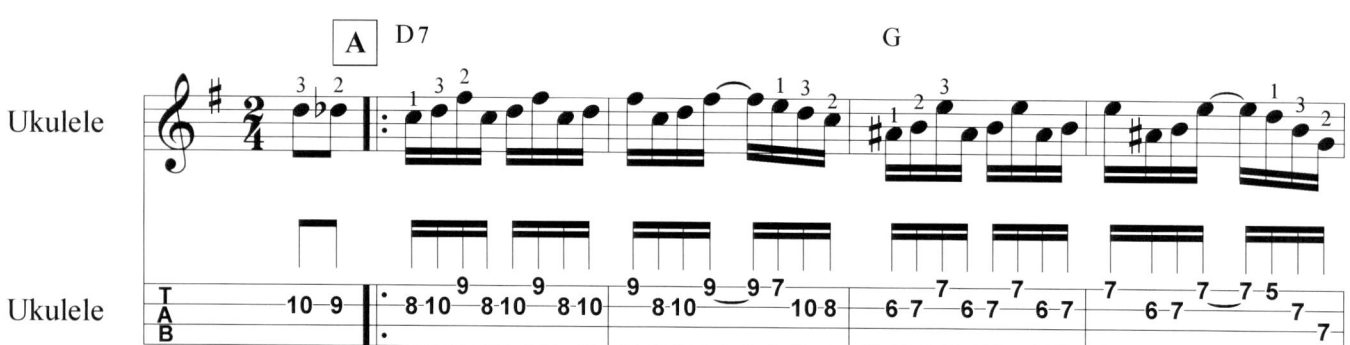
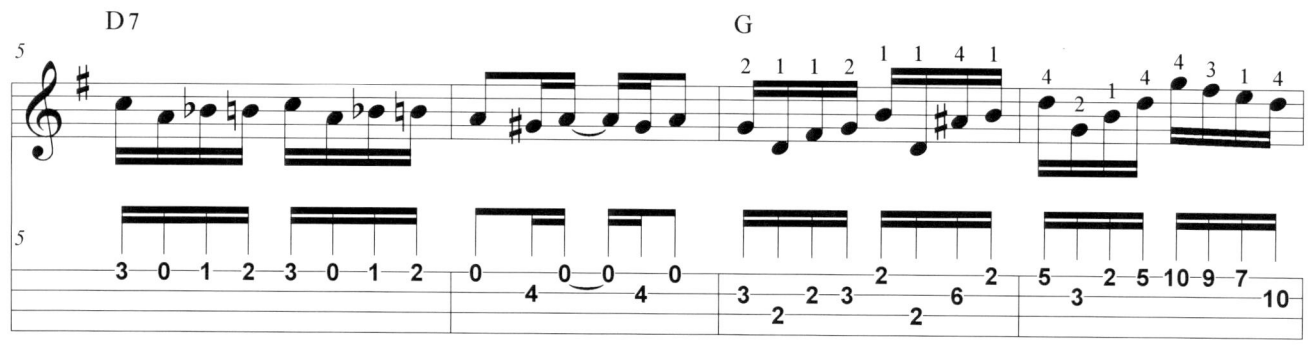
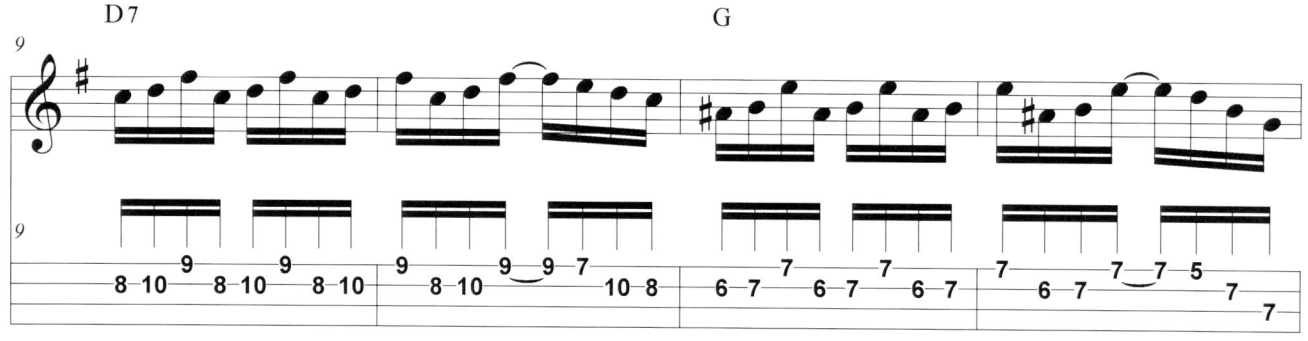
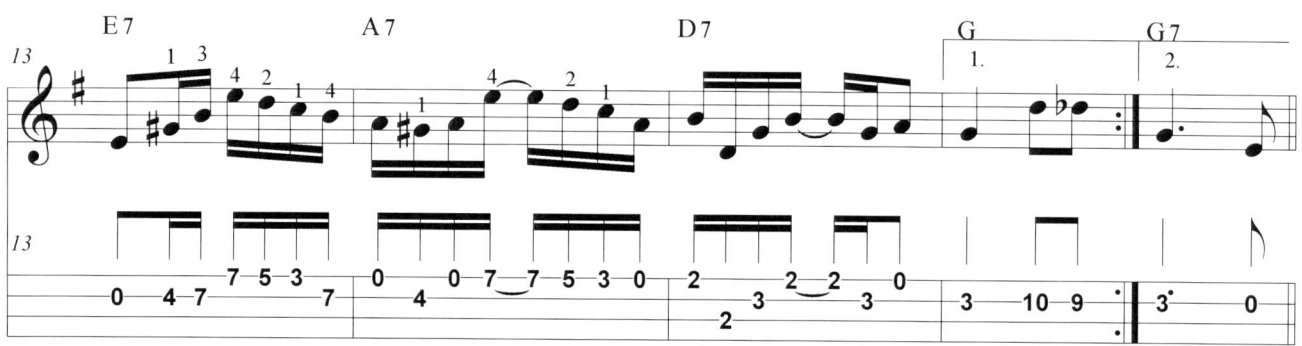

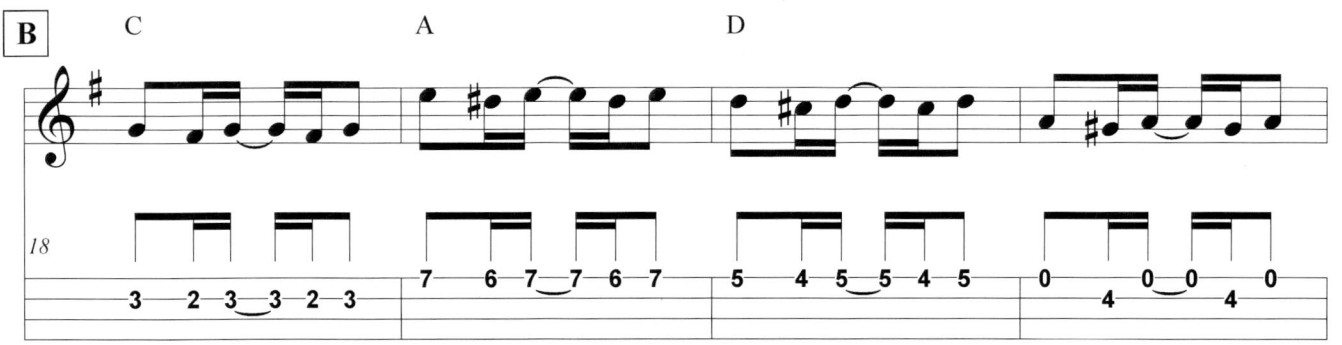
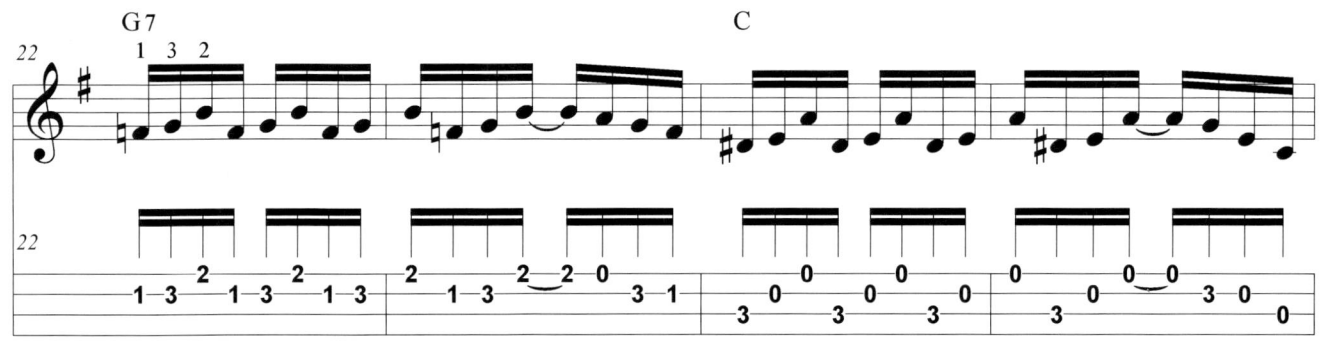
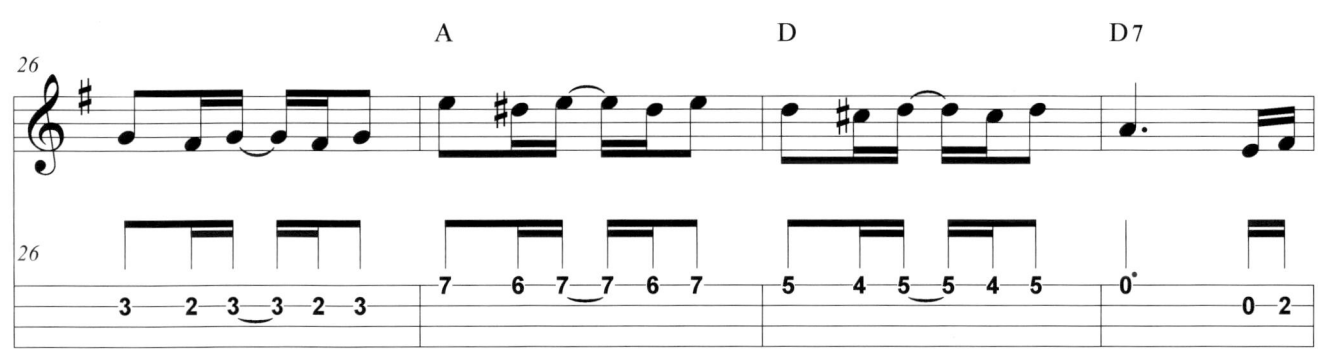
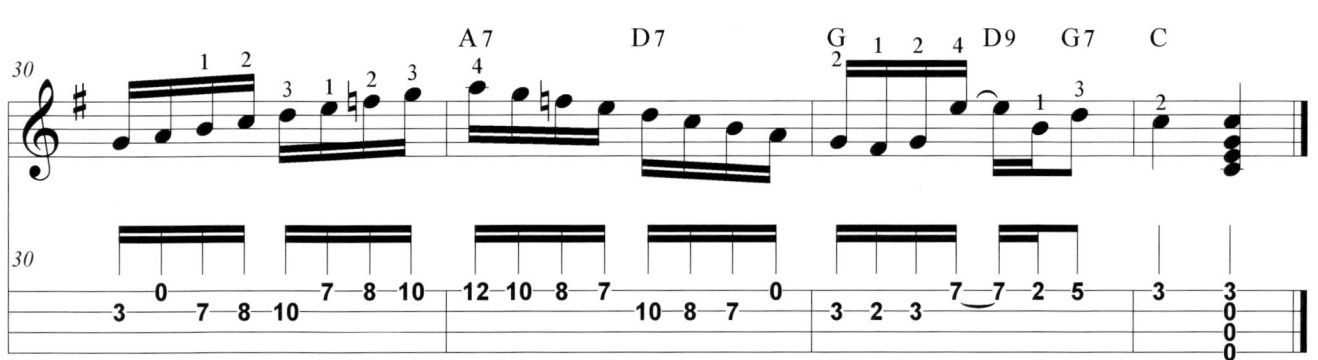

East Tennessee Blues

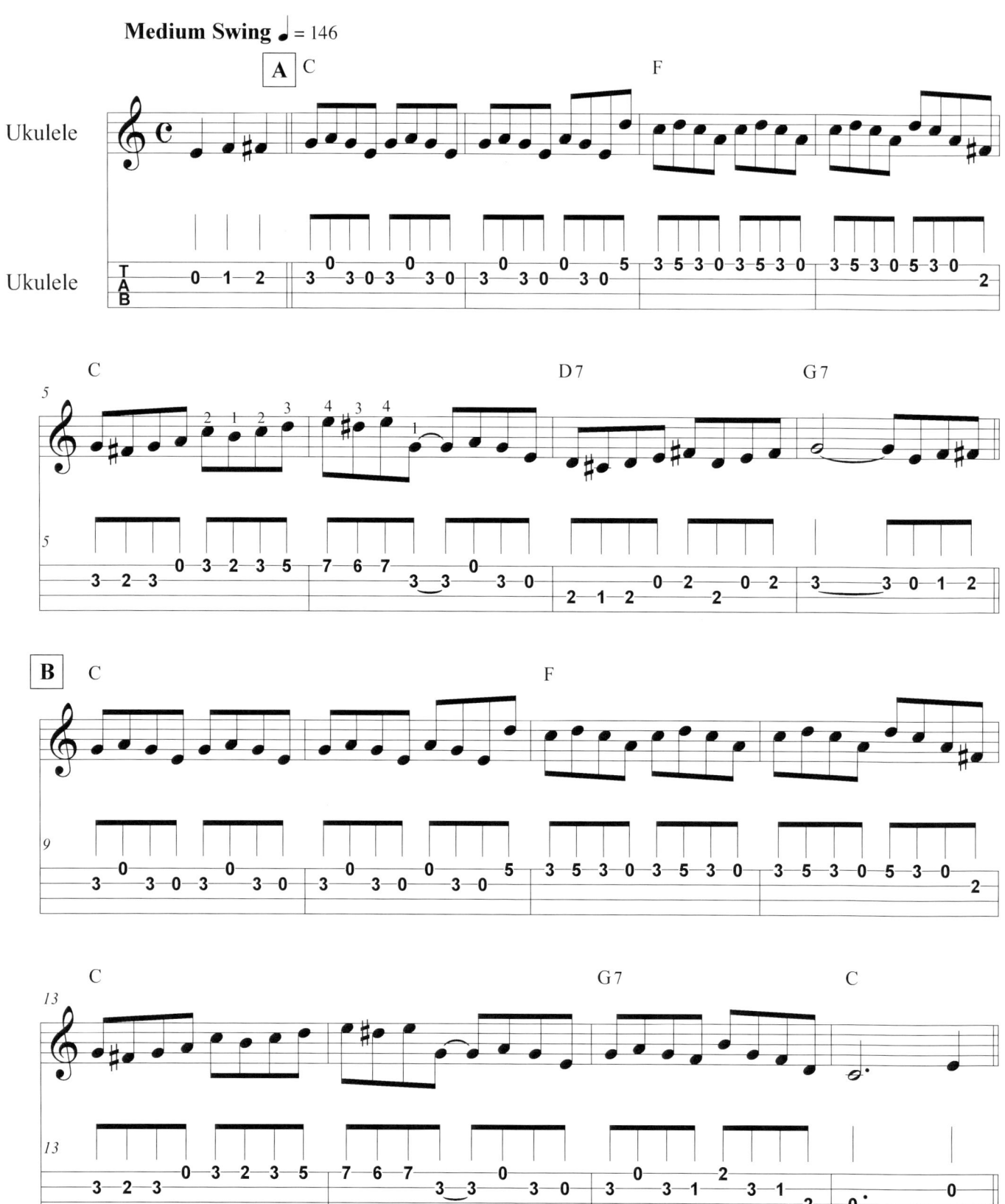

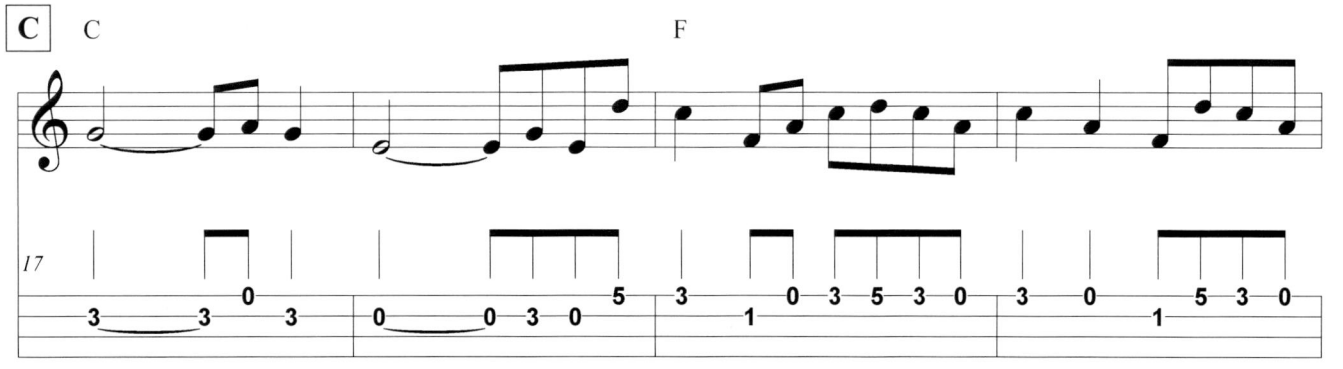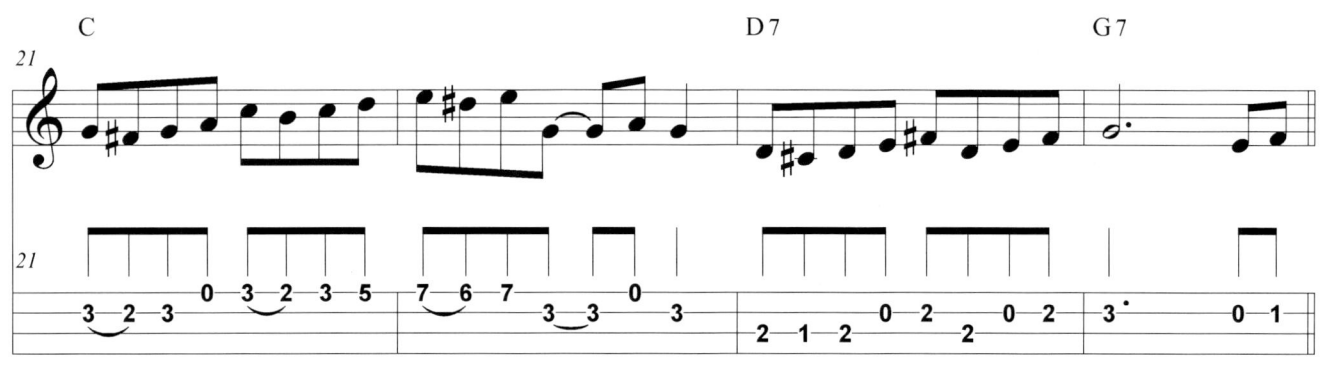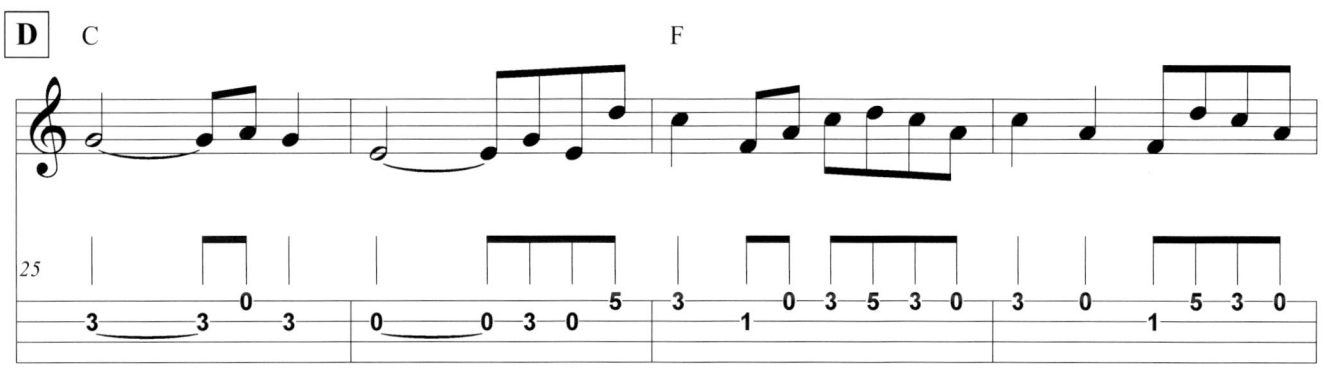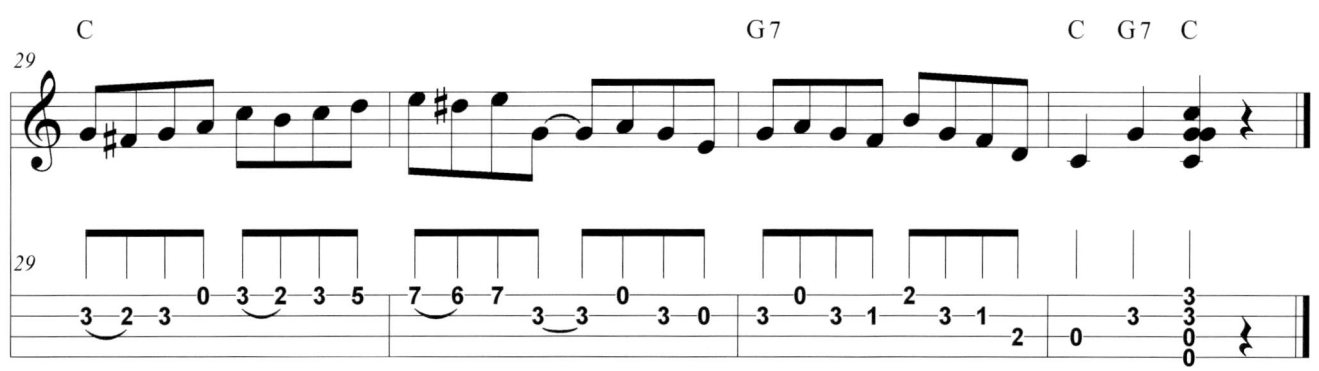

Silver Bell

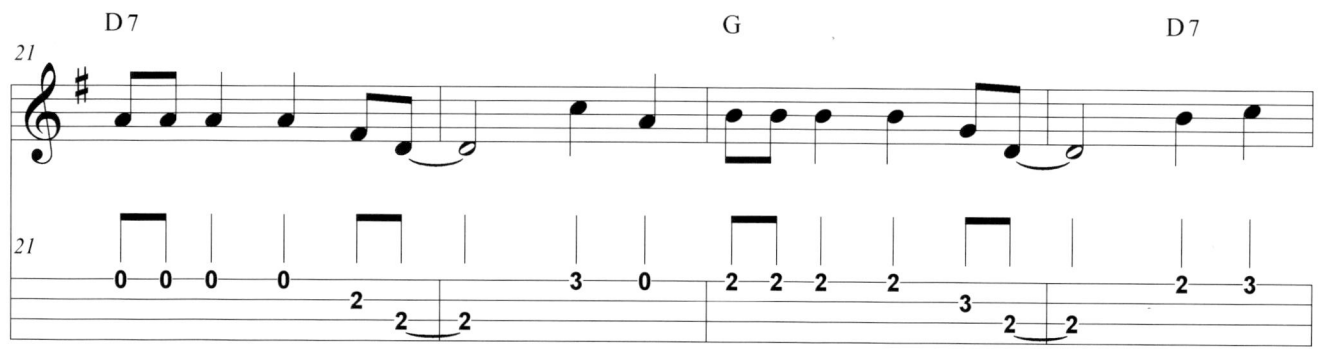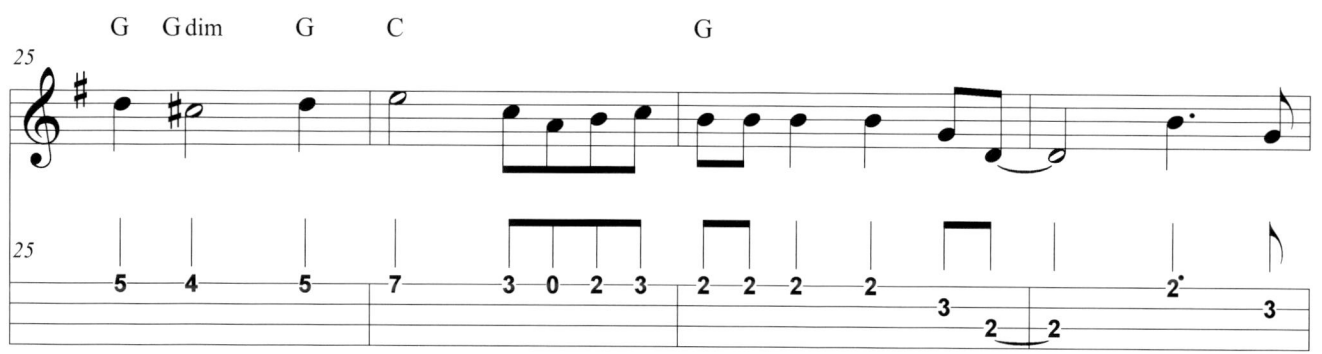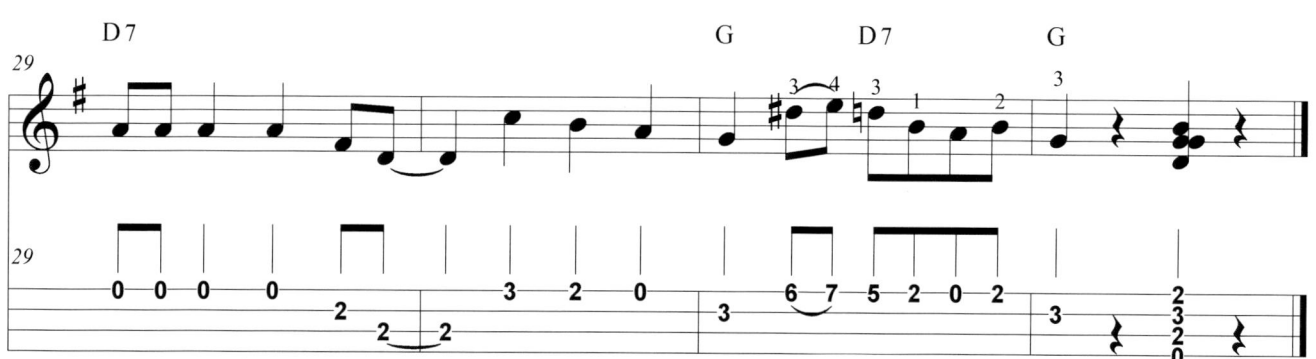

Stone's Rag

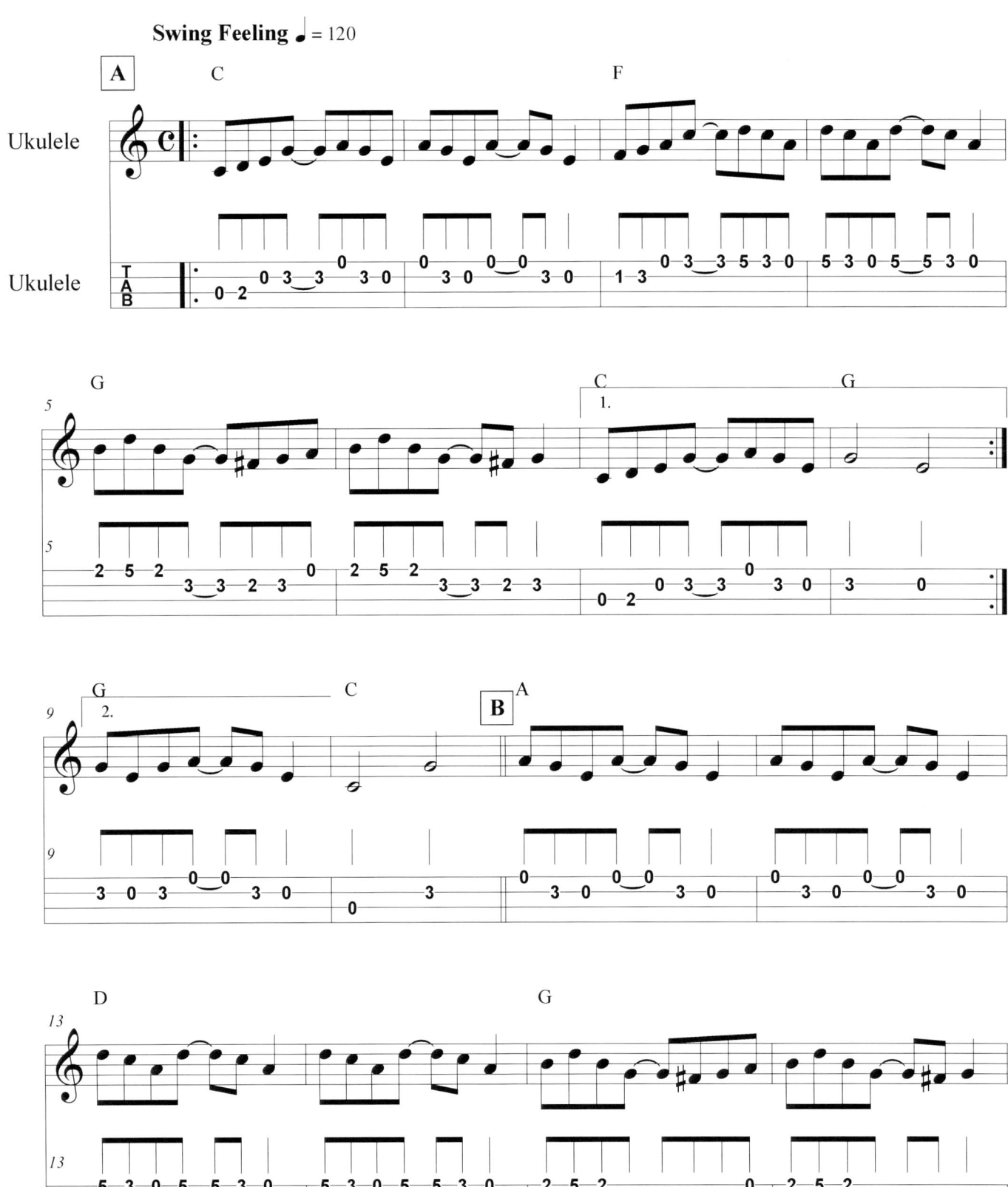

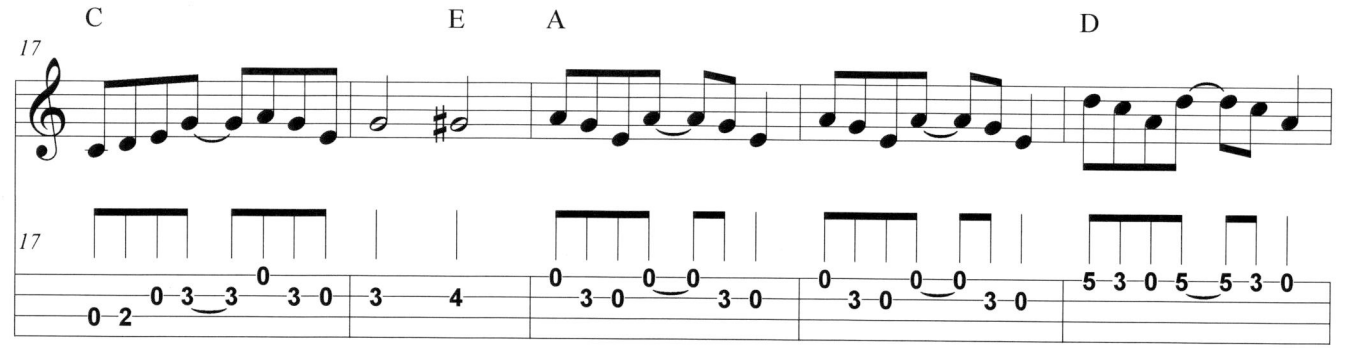
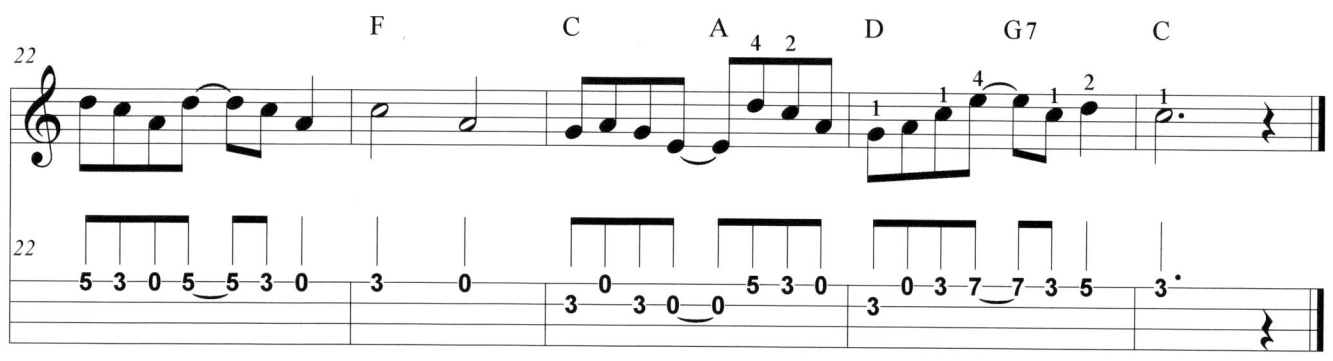

Sweet Lillie

Appalachian Folk Melody

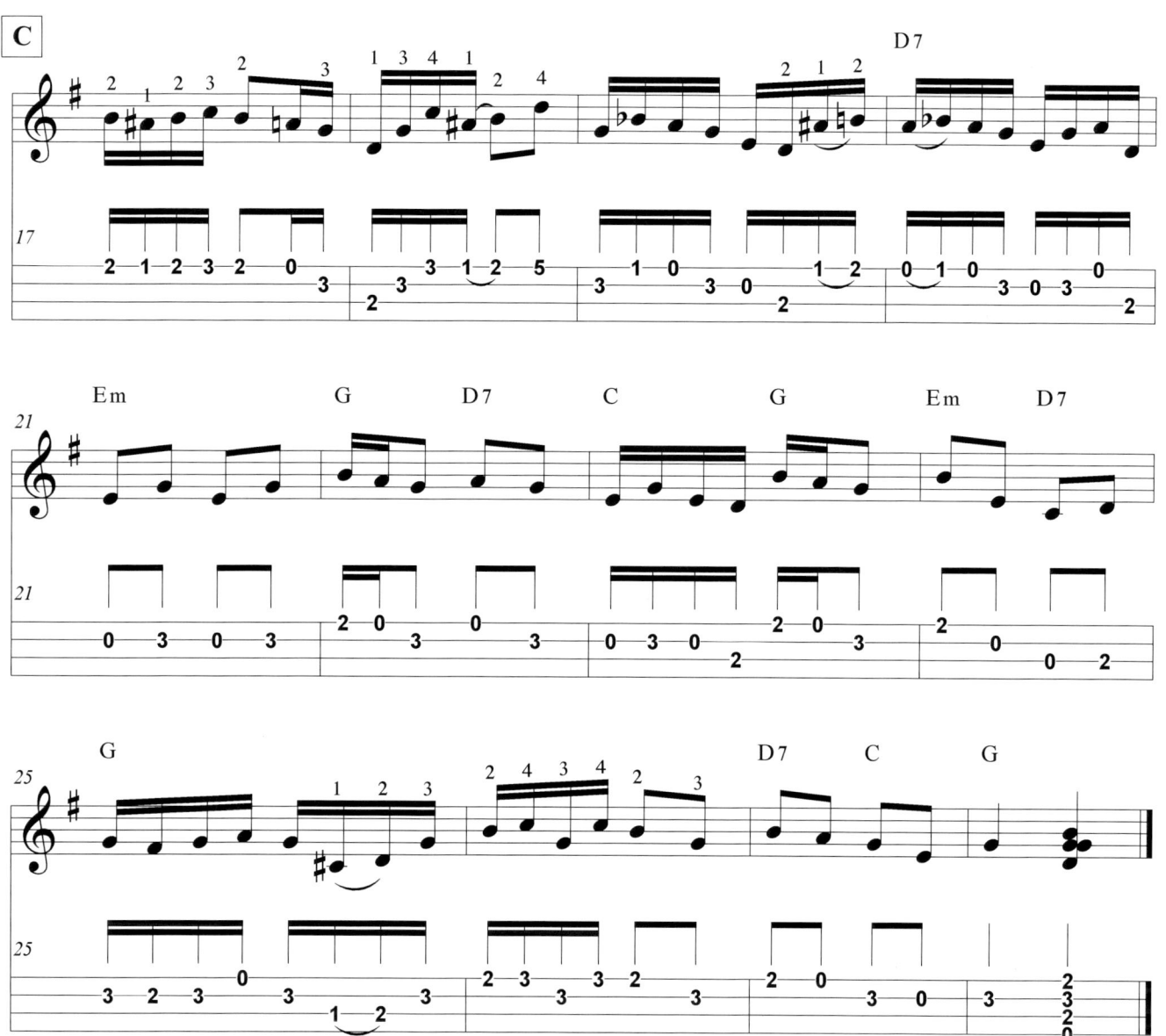

Dixie Breakdown

Lost Indian

Sugar in the Gourd

Jacks Fork Rendezvous

William Bay

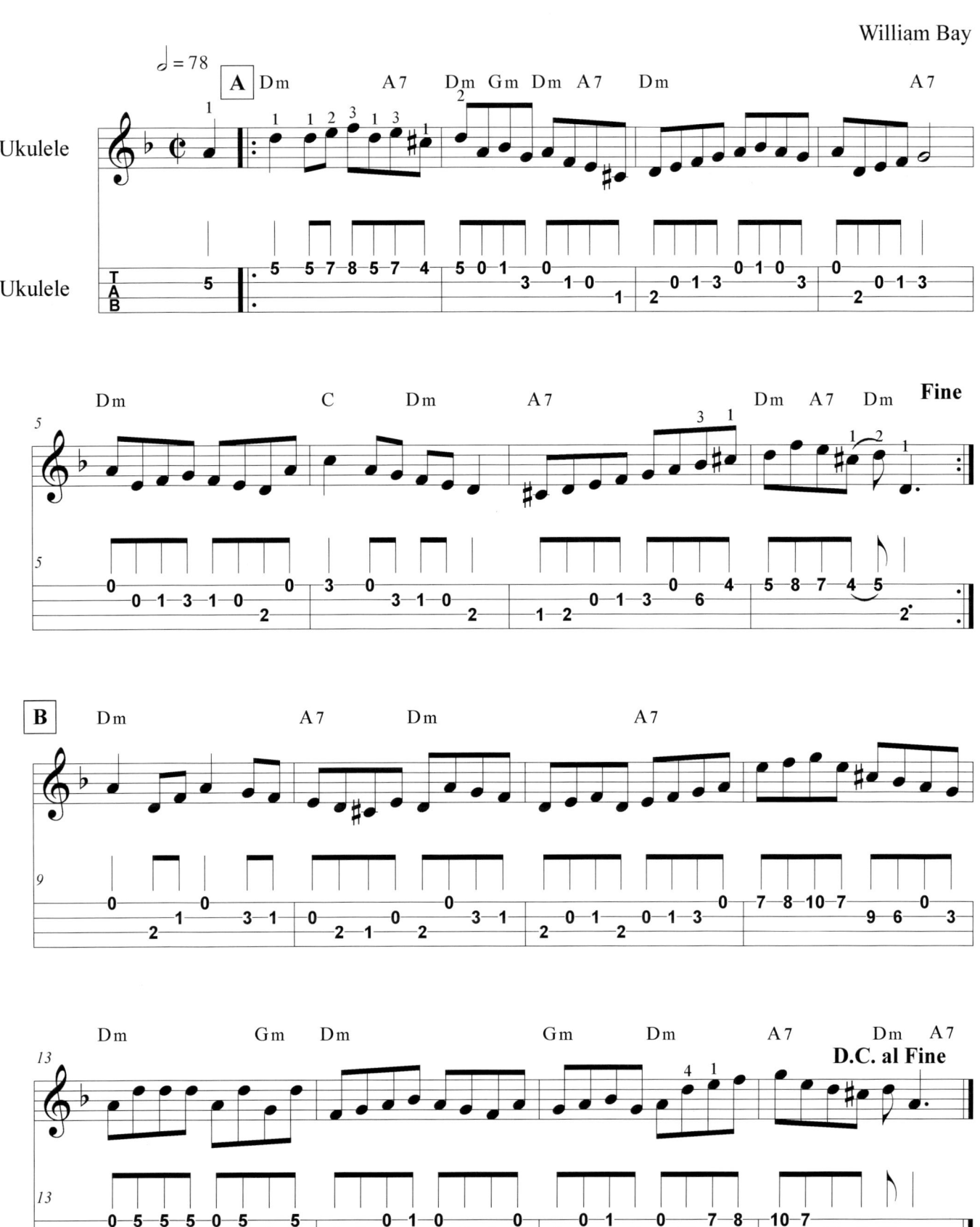

Blanchard's Hornpipe

Bottom of the Punch Bowl Hornpipe

Indian Creek

Brunswick Dance

Cape Cod Reel

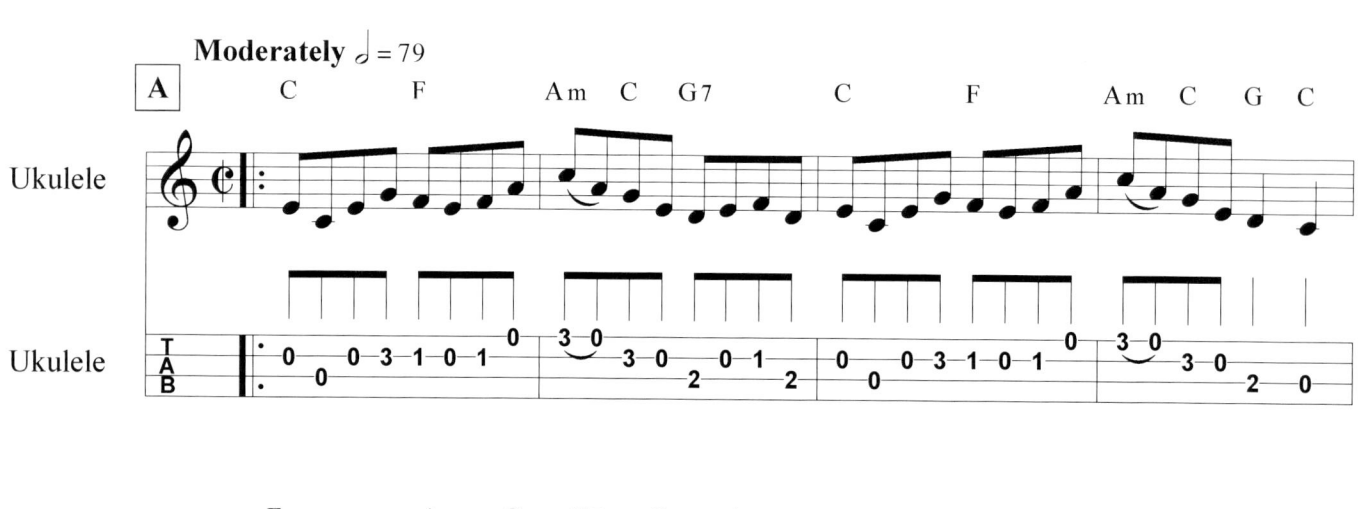
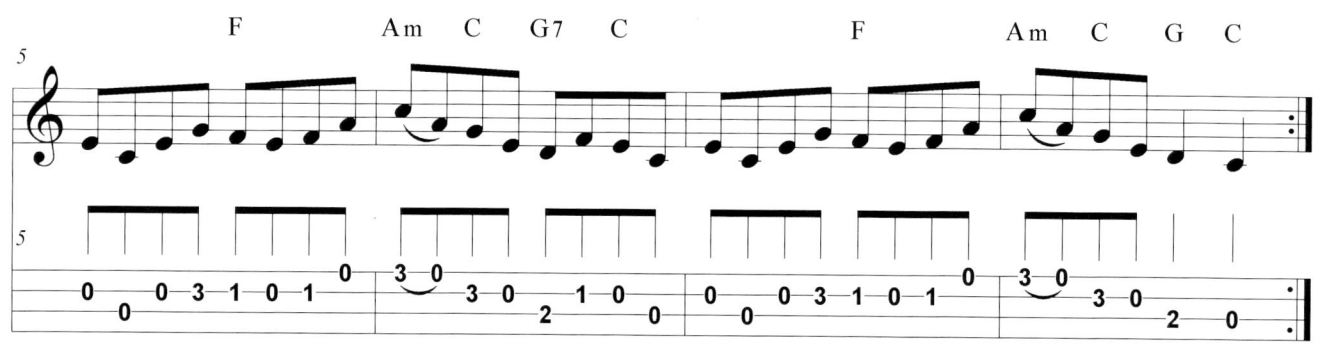
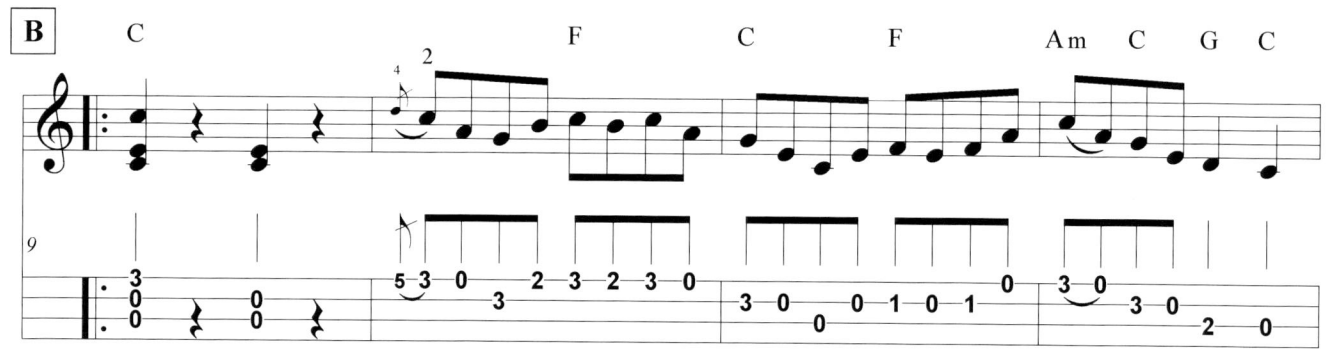
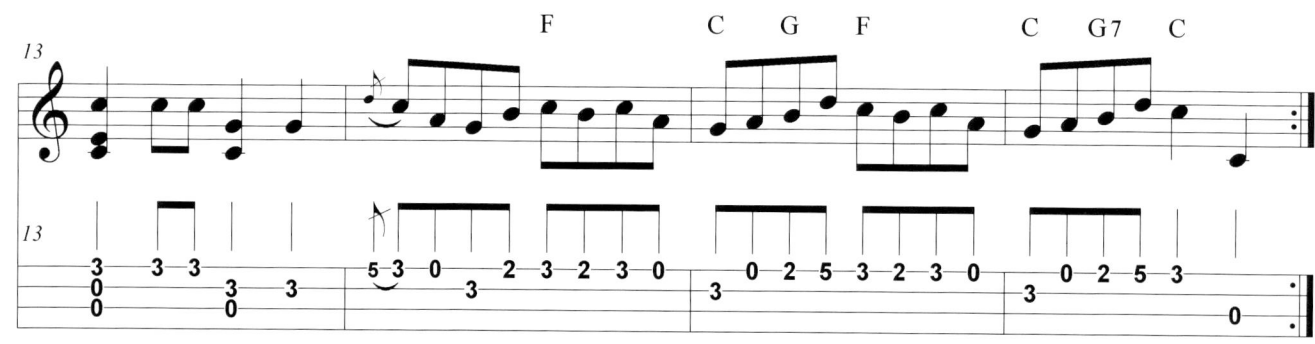

Echo Canyon

William Bay

Catawissa Reel

Devil's Dream

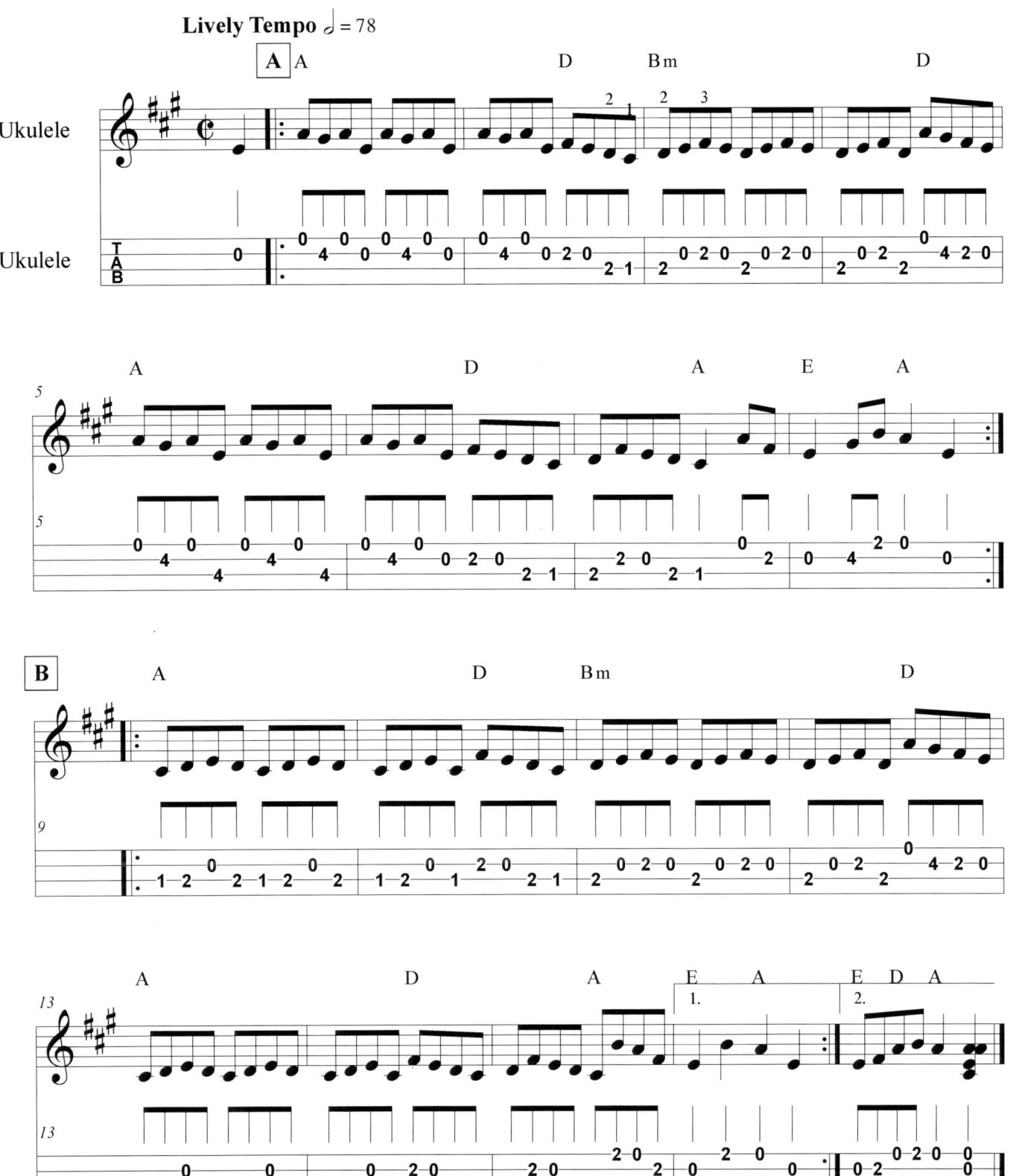

Haul Away, Joe

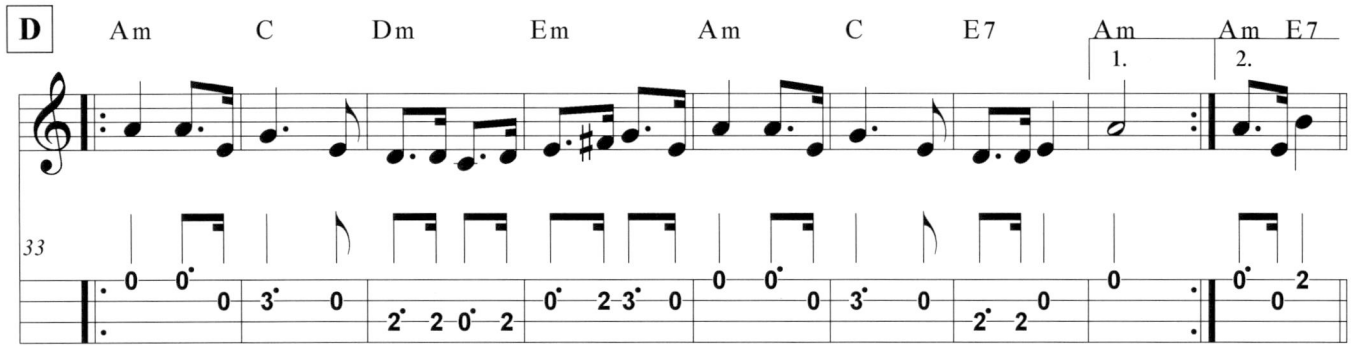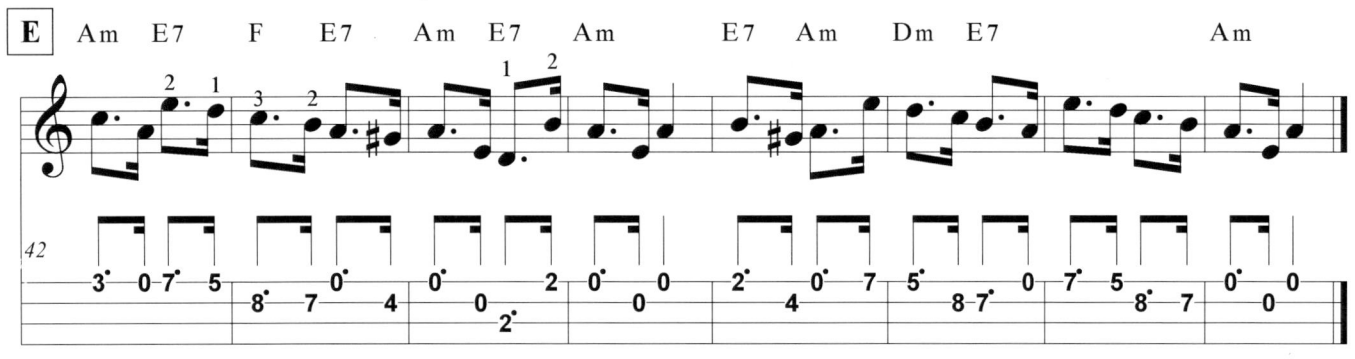

Lady's Fancy

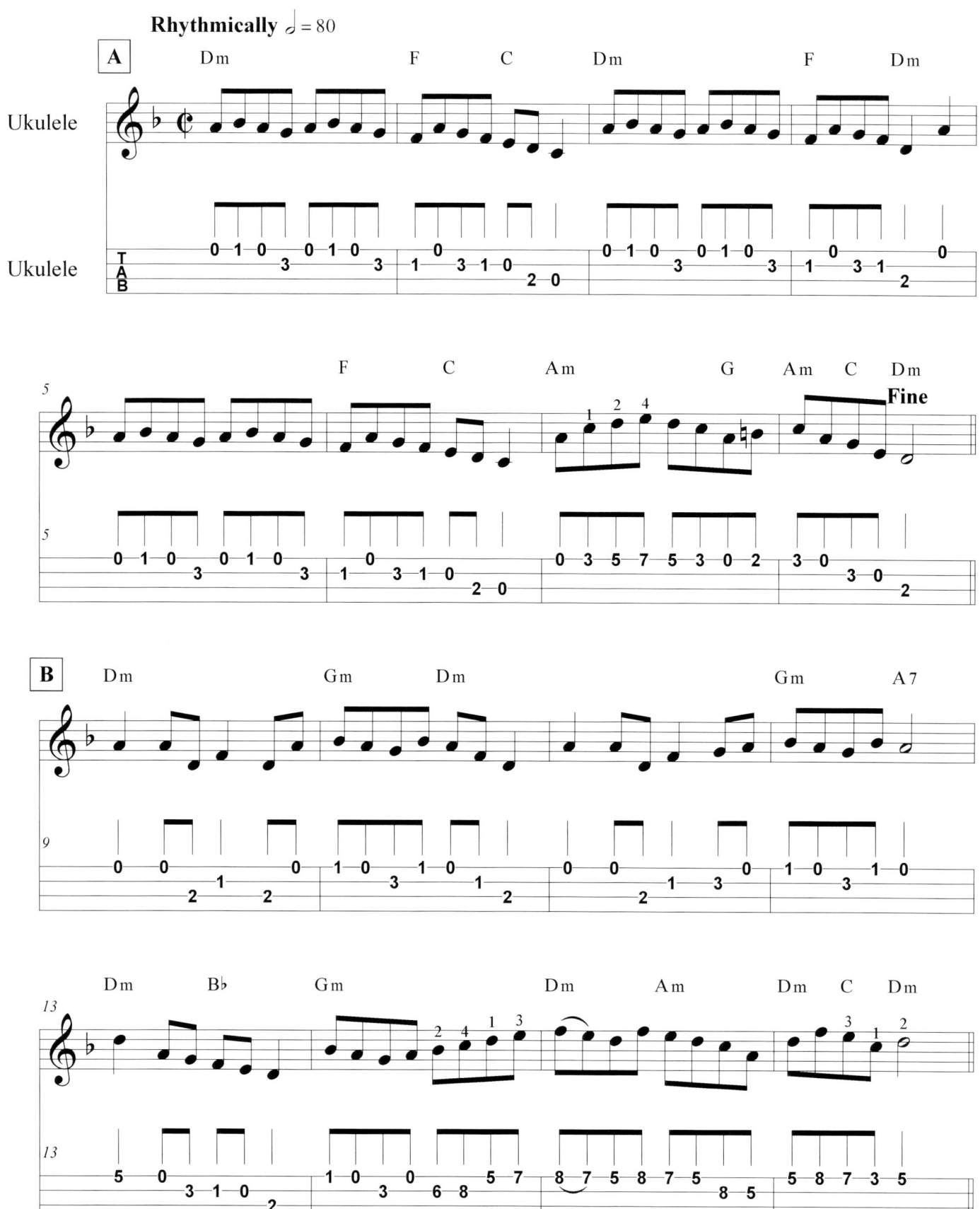

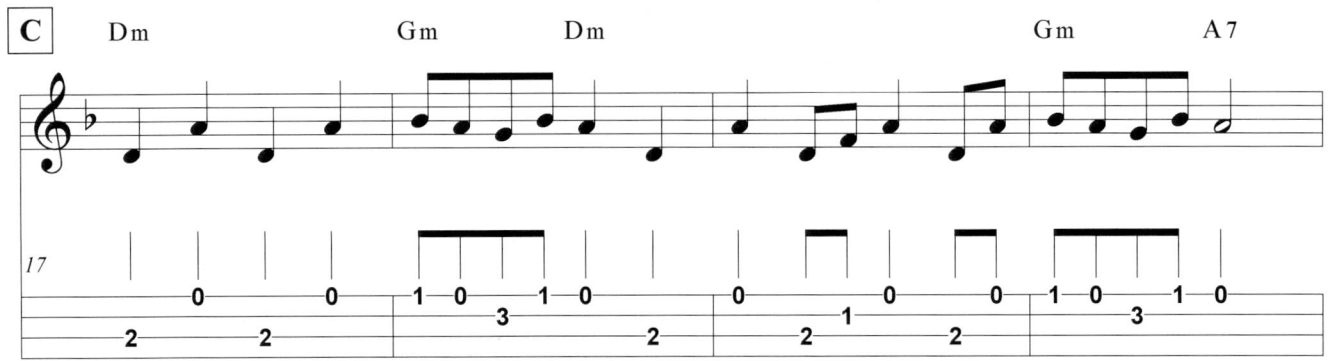
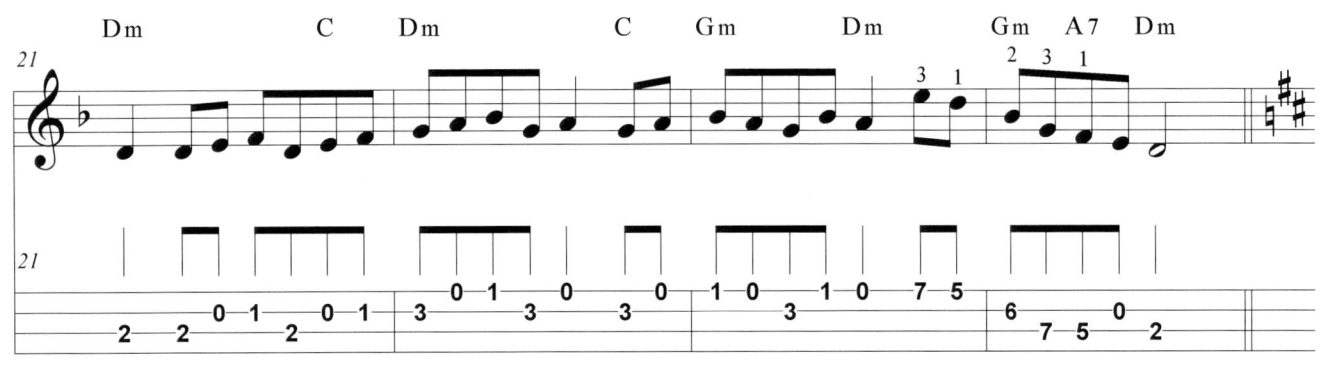
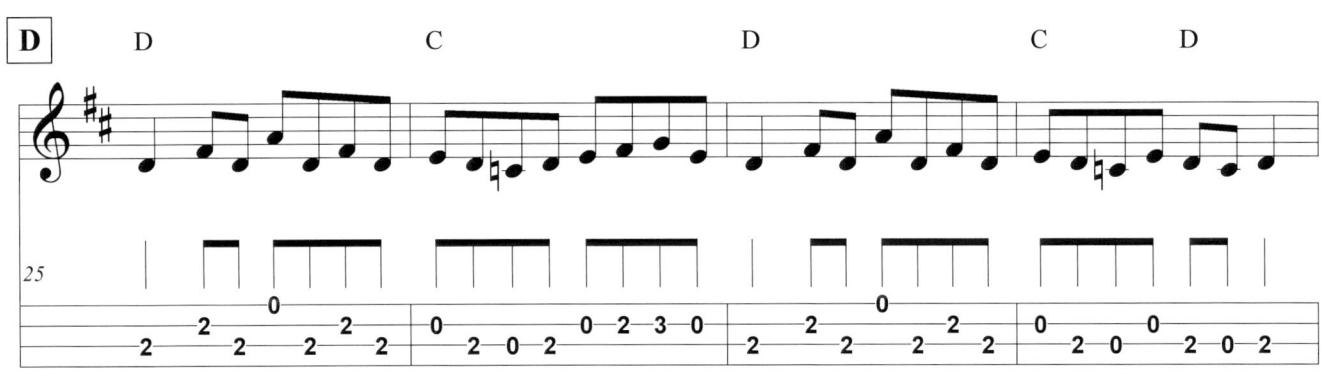
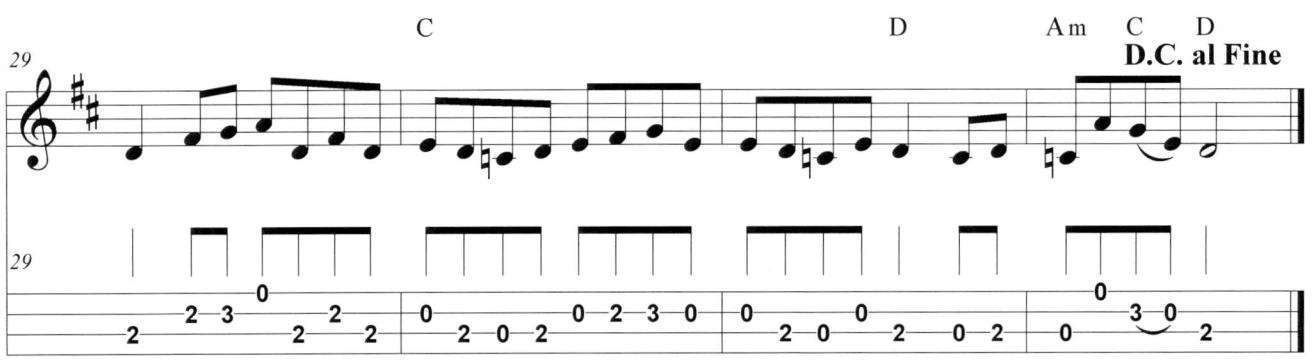

Haste to the Wedding

Hens in the Kitchen

Hooker's Hornpipe

Katie Trail

High Barbaree

London Hornpipe

Maddie's Bonnet

Lonesome River

William Bay

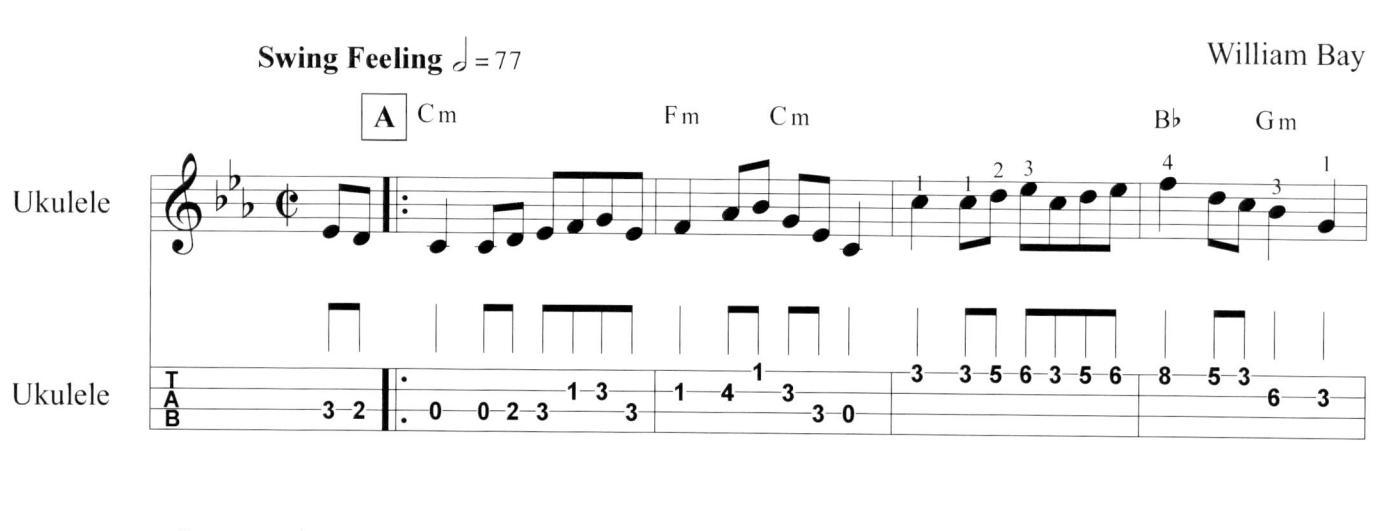
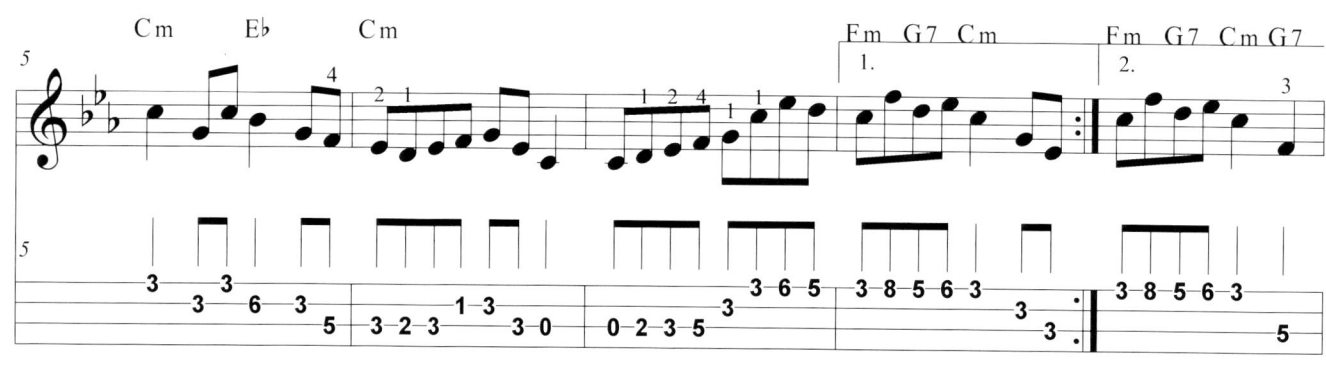
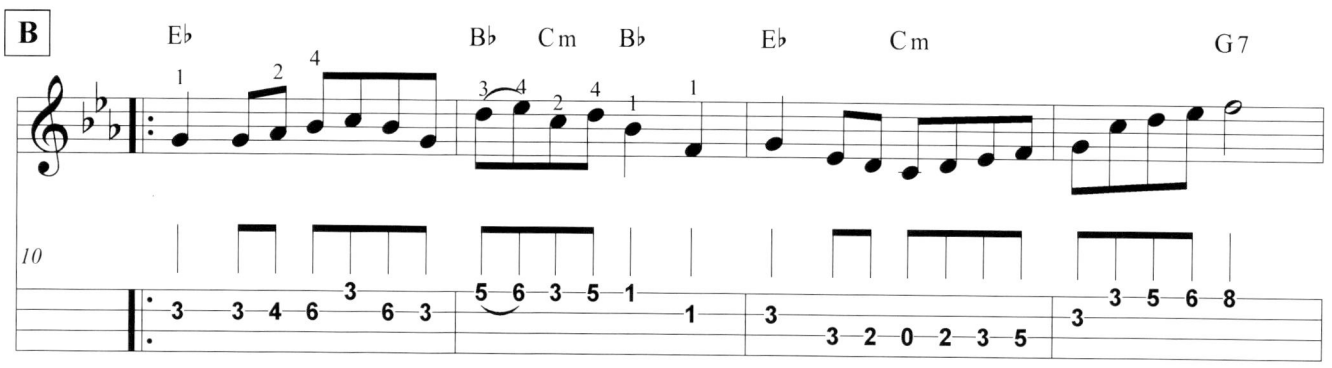
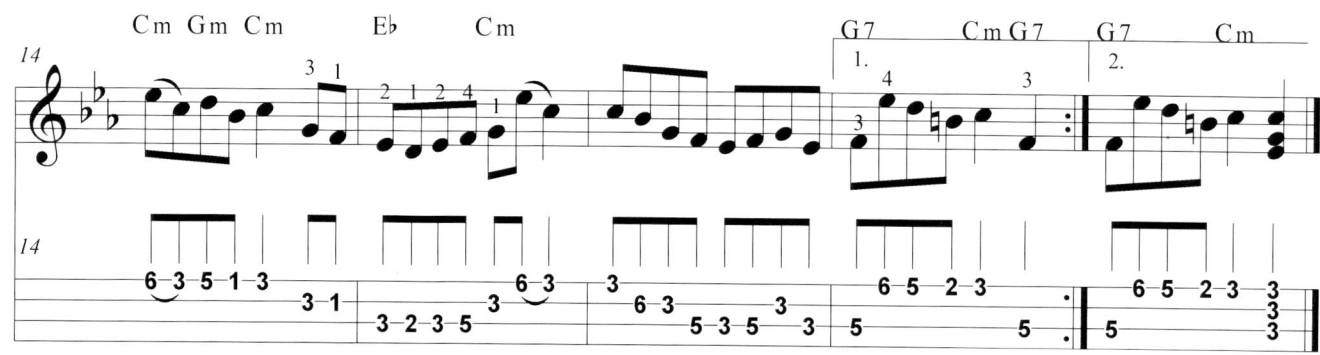

Martha's Cider

Ships are Sailing Reel

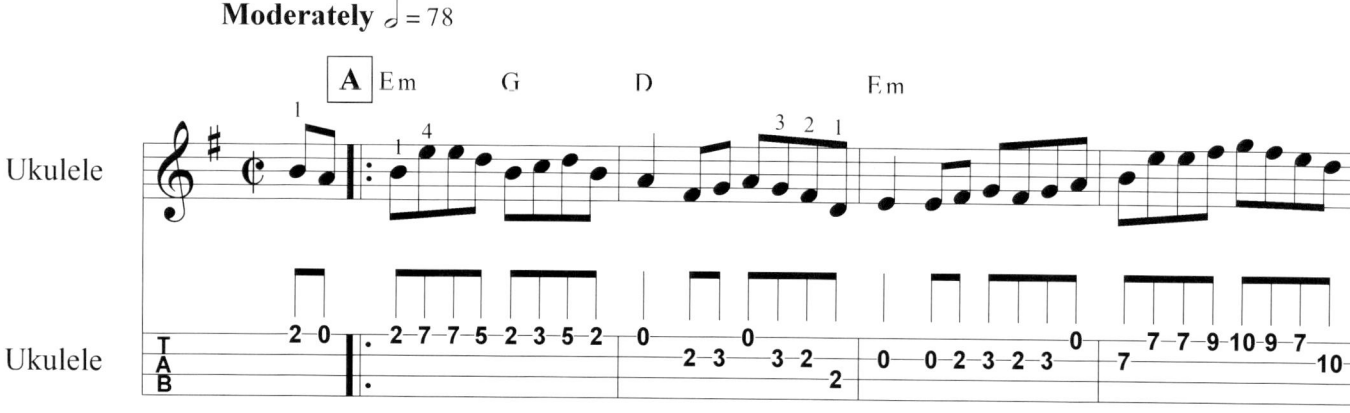
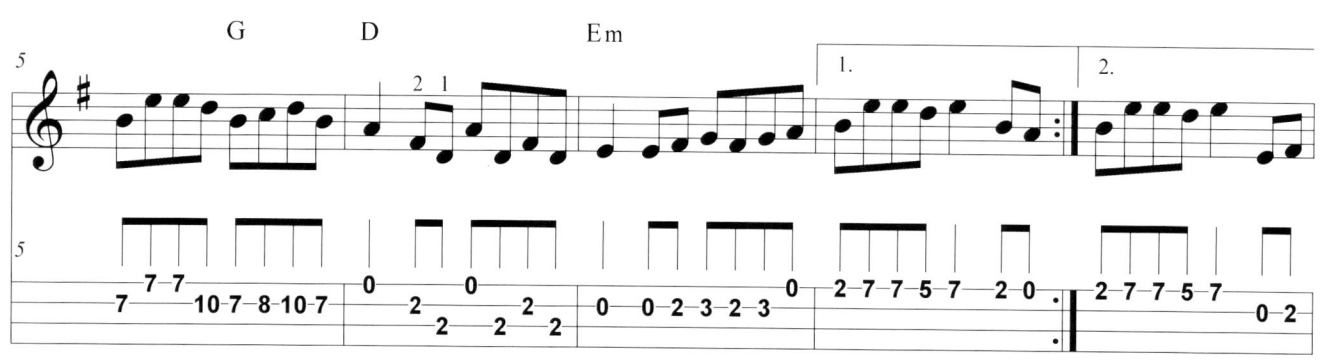
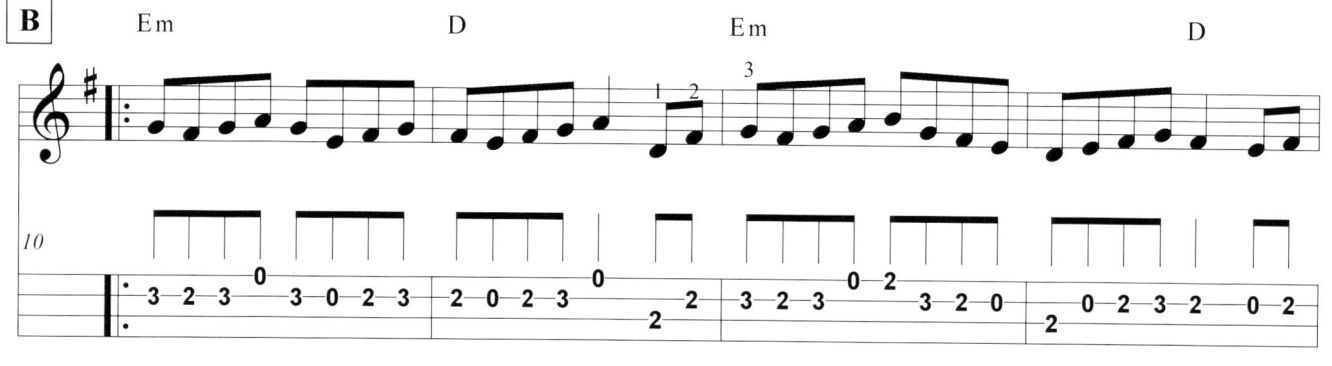
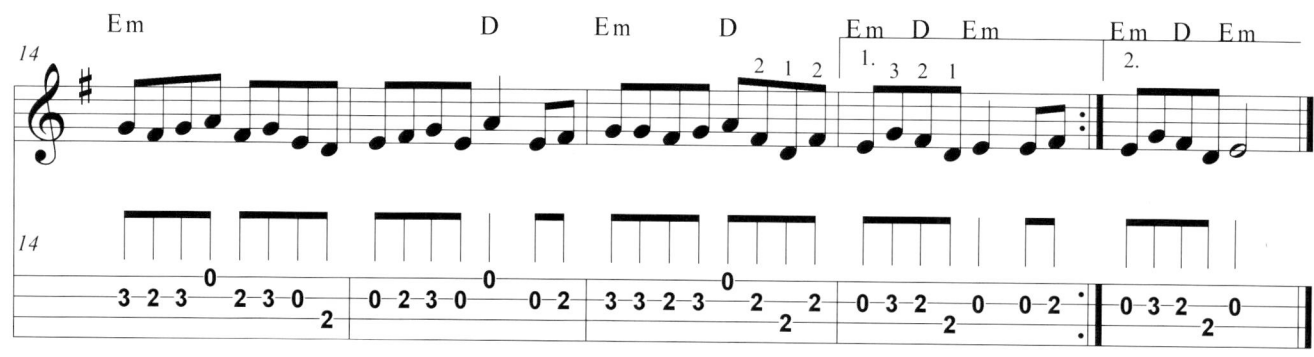

Rickett's Hornpipe

Moderate Swing Tempo ♩ = 77

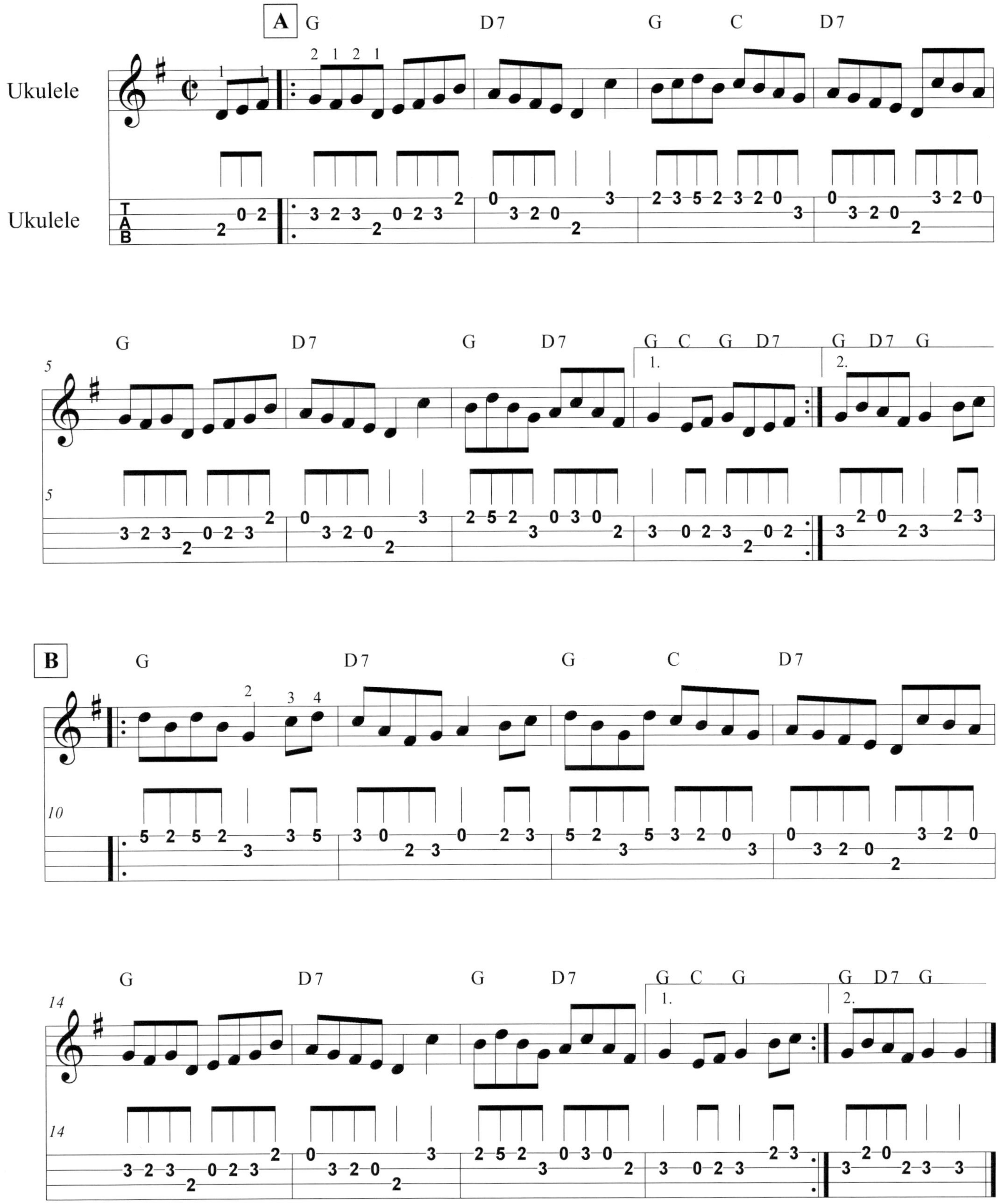

The Wild Mare

Powder Mill

William Bay

American Hornpipe

Other Recommended Mel Bay Ukulele Books

Children's Ukulele Method (Andrews)
Dirt Simple Uke (Carr)
Easy Ukulele Method Book 1 (Dempler)
Easy Ukulele Method Book 2 (Dempler)
First Lessons Fingerstyle Ukulele (Gilewitz)
Fun with the Ukulele (M. Bay)
Fun with Strums: Ukulele (W. Bay)
Learn to Play Fingerstyle Solos for Ukulele (Nelson)
Learn to Play Slack Key 'Ukulele (Nelson)
Modern Ukulele Method Grade 1 (Carr)
Open Tunings for Ukulele (Šárek)
Ukulele for Seniors (Carr)
Ukulele Method (Roy Smeck)
You Can Teach Yourself Uke (W. Bay)
Children's Ukulele Chord Book (Andrews)
Left-Handed Uke Chord Chart (W. Bay)
Left-Handed Ukulele Chords (M. Bay)
Mastering Chord Inversions for Ukulele (Nelson)
Uke Chord Chart (W. Bay)
Ukulele Chords (M. Bay)
Uke Chords Made Easy (W. Bay)
Uke Rhythms: Picking and Strumming Patterns (Driscoll)
Understanding Ukulele Chords (van Renesse)
20 Caribbean Pieces for Ukulele (Carr)
20 Celtic Fingerstyle Uke Tunes (MacKillop)
20 Easy Classical Uke Pieces for Kids (MacKillop)
20 Old Time American Tunes Arranged for Ukulele (MacKillop)
20 Popular Uke Tunes for Kids (MacKillop)
20 Spanish Baroque Pieces by Gaspar Sanz Arranged for Uke (MacKillop)
Children's Songs for Solo Ukulele (Carr)
Classics for Ukulele (Šárek)
Famous Solos and Duets for the Ukulele (King)
Favorite Classical Themes for Ukulele (Coe)
Favorite Fingerstyle Solos for Ukulele (Nelson)
Favorite Old-Time American Songs for Ukulele (Nelson)
Fingerstyle Duets for Ukulele (Nelson)
First Jams: Ukulele (Andrews)
Folk Songs for Solo Ukulele (Carr)
Francisco Tarrega for Ukulele (Šárek)
Gospel Favorites for Solo Ukulele (Carr)
Great Melodies for Solo Ukulele (Carr)
Hawaiian Uke Tunebook (Eidson/Cherednik)

WWW.MELBAY.COM

Other Recommended Mel Bay Ukulele Books

Holiday Favorites for Solo Ukulele (Carr)
Indie Rock Uke (Driscoll)
Leopold Mozart's Notebook for Wolfgang Arranged for Ukulele (Šárek)
Mauro Giuliani arranged for Ukulele Duet (Šárek)
Sacred Music for Ukulele (Dempler)
Songs & Solos for Uke (Eidson/Cherednik)
The Bach Uke Book (MacKillop)
Ukulele Bluegrass Solos (Šárek)
Ukulele Chord Solos in C Tuning (Griffin)
Ukulele Christmas Carols (Andrews)
Ukulele Duets (Carr)
101 Three-Chord Children's Songs for Guitar, Banjo and Uke (McCabe)
101 Three-Chord Country & Bluegrass Songs (McCabe)
101 Three-Chord Songs for Guitar, Banjo and Uke (McCabe)
50 Three-Chord Christmas Songs for Guitar, Banjo and Uke (McCabe)
Favorite Old-Time American Songs for Ukulele (Nelson)
Favorite Uke Tunes (N. Jones)
Fun with Folk Songs (M. Bay)
Sacred Music for Ukulele (Dempler)
Sing and Strum: 7 Hawaiian Favorites for Ukulele (Kimura)
Songs & Solos for Uke (Eidson/Cherednik)
Ten Favorite Hawaiian Songs (Kimura)
The Cat's Meow: Ukulele Favorites from the Roaring Twenties (Whitcomb)
Uke Ballads: A Treasure of 25 Love Songs Old and New (Whitcomb)
Uke Tunes Made Easy (W. Bay)
Ukulele Christmas Carols (Andrews)
Ukulele Heaven: Songs from the Golden Age of the Ukulele (Whitcomb)
Ukulele Jamboree! (Whitcomb)
Ukulele Party (Moore)
Ukulele Picking Tunes - Early Music Gems (Šárek)
Ukulele Picking Tunes - Fun Songs to Play (Šárek)
20 Easy Fingerstyle Studies for Ukulele (MacKillop)
20 Progressive Fingerstyle Studies for Uke (MacKillop)
Chord Melody Method for Uke (Moore)
Hints and Tips for Advanced Ukulele Players (Kimura)
Killer Technique: Ukulele (C. Bay)
Learn to Burn: Uke (Driscoll)
Scales for Soprano Ukulele (Andrews)
Ukulele Anatomy and Mechanics Wall Chart (Lee-Georgescu)
Ukulele Handbook (Richter)
Ukulele Manuscript Book
Ukulele Wall Chart (C. Bay)
Understanding Ukulele Chords (van Renesse)

WWW.MELBAY.COM